Pebble® Plus

Aircraft

Hot Air Balloons

by Mari Schuh

Consulting Editor: Gail Saunders-Smith, PhD

Consultant: Stewart W. Bailey, Curator
Evergreen Aviation & Space Museum
McMinnville, Oregon

CAPSTONE PRESS
a capstone imprint

Pebble Plus is published by Capstone Press,
1710 Roe Crest Drive, North Mankato, Minnesota 56003
www.capstonepub.com

Library of Congress Cataloging-in-Publication Data
Cataloging-in-publication information is on file with the Library of Congress.
978-1-62065-111-7 (library binding)
978-1-4765-1069-9 (eBook PDF)

Editorial Credits
Erika L. Shores, editor; Heidi Thompson, designer; Eric Manske, production specialist

Photo Credits
Dreamstime: Brandon Bourdages, 7; Shutterstock: 501room, 9, Adrian Highes, 19, Alain Lauga, 13, Boykov, 21, dani92026, cover, ermess, 15, italianestro, 17, Luciano Mottula, 11, Nicolas Raymond, 5

Artistic Effects
Shutterstock: New Line

The author dedicates this book to St. Lucy Parish School in Racine, Wisconsin.

Note to Parents and Teachers

The Aircraft set supports national science standards related to science, technology, and society. This book describes and illustrates hot air balloons. The images support early readers in understanding the text. The repetition of words and phrases helps early readers learn new words. This book also introduces early readers to subject-specific vocabulary words, which are defined in the Glossary section. Early readers may need assistance to read some words and to use the Table of Contents, Glossary, Read More, Internet Sites, and Index sections of the book.

Printed in China
092012   006934LEOS13

Table of Contents

Hot Air Balloons

Hot air balloons float

like clouds across the sky.

Let's get carried away!

Most hot air balloons are

at least 50 feet (15 meters) tall.

That's taller than a house!

Parts of Hot Air Balloons

Hot air balloons are made of nylon. This fabric is light and strong.

People stand in

a wicker basket attached

under the balloon.

A very large balloon carries

as many as 16 people.

Whoosh!

Burners burn propane gas
under the balloon.
The burning gas heats air
inside the balloon.

What They Do

Hot air balloons float

with the wind.

They go where

the wind pushes them.

Pilots can make

the balloon fly higher.

They burn more gas.

Hotter air makes

the balloon rise higher.

Pilots can make

the balloon fly lower.

They burn less gas.

Pilots can also open a vent

to let out hot air.

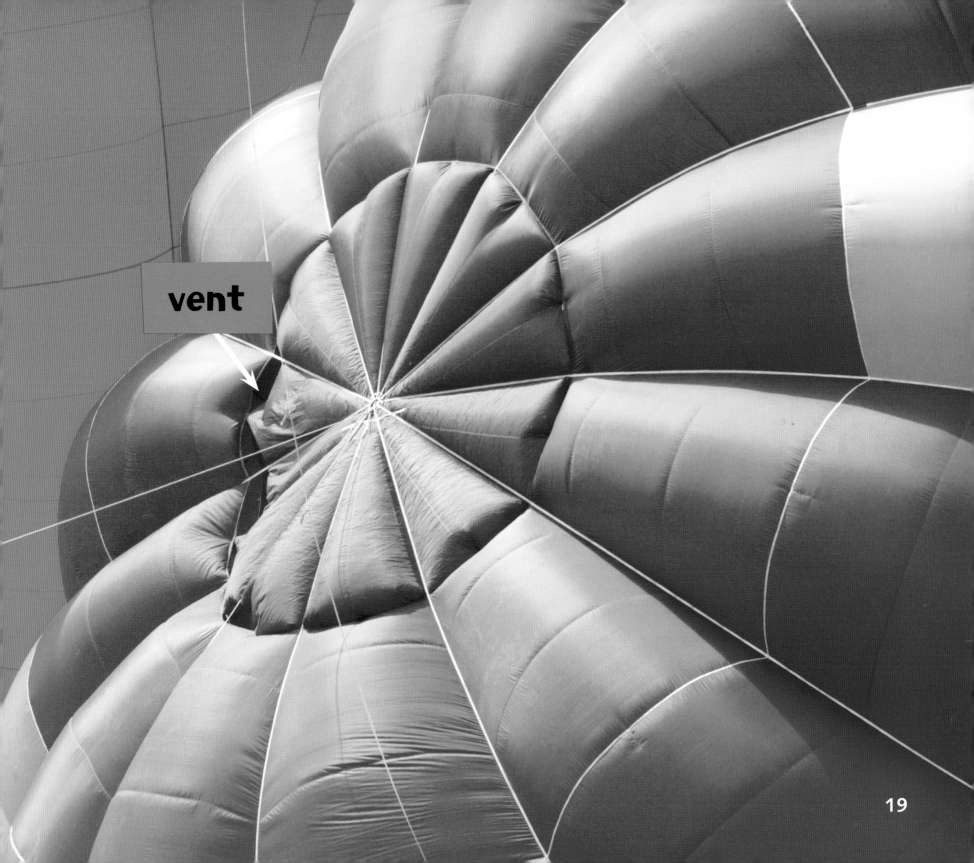

vent

19

Up, Up, and Away!

People enjoy watching
hot air balloon races.
Which balloon will travel
the farthest?

Glossary

burner—a device that makes a flame

nylon—a very strong material that is used to make cloth

pilot—the person who flies hot air balloons or other aircraft

propane—a colorless gas burned for fuel

vent—an opening at the top of a hot air balloon

wicker—a strong but flexible material made of wood

Read More

Hanson, Anders. *Let's Go by Hot Air Balloon*. Let's Go! Edina, Minn.: Abdo Pub. Co., 2008.

Hicks, Kelli L. *Hot Air Ballooning*. Action Sports. Vero Beach, Fla.: Rourke Pub. 2010.

Masters, Nancy Robinson. *Hot Air Balloon*. Community Connections: How Does It Fly? Ann Arbor, Mich.: Cherry Lake Pub., 2012.

Internet Sites

FactHound offers a safe, fun way to find Internet sites related to this book. All of the sites on FactHound have been researched by our staff.

Here's all you do:

Visit *www.facthound.com*

Type in this code: 9781620651117

Super-cool stuff! Check out projects, games and lots more at
www.capstonekids.com

Index

Word Count: 146
Grade: 1
Early-Intervention Level: 17